Basketball Superstar Kevin Durant

by Jon M. Fishman

BUMBA BOOKS™

LERNER PUBLICATIONS ◆ MINNEAPOLIS

Note to Educators

Throughout this book, you'll find critical-thinking questions. These can be used to engage young readers in thinking critically about the topic and in using the text and photos to do so.

Lerner Publications Company
A division of Lerner Publishing Group, Inc.
241 First Avenue North
Minneapolis, MN 55401 USA

For reading levels and more information, look up this title at www.lernerbooks.com.

Main body text set in Helvetica Textbook Com Roman 23/49.
Typeface provided by Linotype AG.

Library of Congress Cataloging-in-Publication Data

Names: Fishman, Jon M., author.
Title: Basketball superstar Kevin Durant / by Jon M. Fishman.
Description: Minneapolis, MN : Lerner Publications, [2019] | Series: Bumba books. Sports superstars | Includes
    bibliographical references and index. | Audience: Age 4–7. | Audience: K to Grade 3.
Identifiers: LCCN 2018040877 (print) | LCCN 2018048329 (ebook) | ISBN 9781541557383 (eb pdf) |
    ISBN 9781541557369 (lb : alk. paper)
Subjects: LCSH: Durant, Kevin, 1988– Juvenile literature. | Basketball players—United States—Biography—
    Juvenile literature. | African American basketball players—United States—Biography—Juvenile literature.
Classification: LCC GV884.D868 (ebook) | LCC GV884.D868 F57 2019 (print) | DDC 796.323092 [B]—dc23

LC record available at https://lccn.loc.gov/2018040877

Manufactured in the United States of America
1-46149-45948-11/15/2018

Table of Contents

Tall Superstar

Kevin Durant plays for the Golden

State Warriors.

He is a great basketball player.

Kevin loved to play basketball as a kid.

He was taller than other players.

How does being tall help a basketball player?

Kevin spent lots of time at a gym.

He became a better basketball

player.

Kevin played basketball in college.

He stayed in college for one year.

Kevin joined the Seattle SuperSonics.

He scored the most points on the team.

Why do basketball players try to score points?

13

The SuperSonics moved to

Oklahoma City.

They became the Oklahoma

City Thunder.

Fans in Oklahoma City

loved Kevin.

He helped the team win.

Next, Kevin joined the

Golden State Warriors.

He helped the team become

champions.

Kevin and his team are the best.

They may become champions

again!

Basketball Gear

jersey

DURANT

35

shoes

shorts

basketball

Picture Glossary

champions

winners of the top prize

college

a school after high school

fans

people who like a sport

gym

a building where people play sports

Read More

Fishman, Jon M. *Basketball Superstar Stephen Curry*. Minneapolis: Lerner Publications, 2019.

Flynn, Brendan. *Basketball Time!* Minneapolis: Lerner Publications, 2017.

Rebman, Nick. *Basketball*. Lake Elmo, MN: Focus Readers, 2019.

Index

Photo Credits

Image credits: Matteo Marchi/Getty Images, p. 4; Jonathan Ferrey/Getty Images, pp. 6, 10, 23; TPG/Getty Images, pp. 8, 9, 23; Sporting News Archive/Getty Images, p. 12; Icon Sports Wire/Getty Images, p. 15; J Pat Carter/Stringer/Getty Images, pp. 16, 17, 23; Gregory Shamus/Getty Images, pp. 18, 22, 23; Jamie Sabau/Getty Images, pp. 20, 21; Dan Thornberg/EyeEm/Getty Images, p. 22; NAKphotos/Getty Images, p. 22.

Cover Image: Ethan Miller/Getty Images.